www.keoshasathbooks.com

Keosha Sath Books

P.O. Box 62,

Monrovia, MD, 21770

Library of Congress Control Number: 2020920495

ISBN: 978-1-73549-330-5

Printed in the United States

Baby: Mommy why do we need a passport?

Mommy: So that you can confirm your country of origin, be able to travel outside of the country, and return to your irth country safely.

Baby: Mommy look what I found, a pink grasshopper!

Mommy: Yes, the pink grasshopper is called a katydid, and they sometimes eat fruit.

Baby: I like the color of the katydid.

Baby: Mommy look! There are so many orange and black butterflies flying around!

Mommy: They're called monarch butterflies, and they migrate to Mexico to stay warm. They're important because they help pollinate the wild flowers. Butterflies do not have teeth; they drink their food with a straw-like tongue.

Baby: I like the color of the butterflies.

Baby: Mommy look! There's a hole inside of the ocean!

Mommy: That hole in the water used to be a cave before it filled with water. The hole is more than 400 feet deep. Scuba divers love to explore the great blue hole.

Baby: I like the color of the water.

Baby: Mommy look! There's a lizard in the tree!

Mommy: That's an anole lizard. They're green and have a layer of extra skin on their necks. Anole lizards are nice to children in Barbados, and they like to climb trees.

Baby: I like the color of the anole.

Baby: Mommy what are they making?

Mommy: In Ghana, they make shea butter from the nuts of the shea tree. Ghanian women knead the shea mixture until it thickens. Shea butter is good for moisturizing hair and protecting skin from ultraviolent radiation.

Baby: I like the color of the shea butter.

Baby: Mommy what are those pink birds called?

Mommy: They are called flamingos. Flamingos are found in the Galapagos Islands and they are pink because of the amount of algae that they eat. The algae they eat contains a pigment called carotene. Carotene is also found in sweet potatoes and carrots.

Baby: I like the color of the flamingos.

Baby: Mommy look, rainbow-colored sandwiches!

Mommy: A macaron is a sandwich cookie made out of sugar, egg whites, and food coloring. They can be made into many different flavors and colors.

Baby: Mommy can I have a purple one?

Baby: Mommy, what are those colorful dresses called?

Mommy: In Bangladesh, women wear sarees to enhance their beauty. It takes at least one month to weave them out of silk and cotton thread.

Baby: I love all of the different colored sarees.

Baby: Mommy look! There are red flowers in my tea!

Mommy: In Cambodia, they put red hibiscus flowers in their tea to help keep them cool in the very hot climate.

Baby: I love the color of the hibiscus flowers.

Baby: Mommy, I want to start a nail polish business!

Mommy: That is wonderful! How did you come up with that idea?

Baby: I want to make the colors we saw around the world.
Will you and Daddy help me?

Colors of the World

Business Route

Get Inspired

Choose a name

Find your target audience

Start a social media presence

Register your LLC

Obtain an EIN Tax identifier

Obtain business license and permits

Hire a registered agent

Open a business account

Company address

Create a website for sales

THE END

www.ingramcontent.com/pod-product-compliance
Lightning Source LLC
Chambersburg PA
CBHW040258100426
42811CB00011B/1308